Lorikeet's Invaded by Furry Beasts
Second Edition

Rainbow Lorikeets are so full of life, their fun-loving, mischievous nature is captivating.

This story, the sixth in the Lorikeet's Book Series for young readers, is based on a family of Lorikeets who meet some unruly fluffy visitors in the garden.

This story is dedicated to Karmilla, our Golden Labrador who gave us fourteen and a half years of loyalty and unconditional love.

Through my words and the creative vision of Lillian Falzon, whose illustrations brought these characters to life, I hope you enjoy a peek into the adventures of this quirky, colourful family.

It's a sunny afternoon, the sky is mostly blue. A couple of grey clouds are threatening to burst into rain. The wind blows them away as quickly as they appear.

Lawrence, Loretta and their family of Rainbow Lorikeets fly into the garden to feed on the sunflower seeds.

Royce, Rosanna and their Lorikeet chicks are there already enjoying the excellent conditions and a meal they know is waiting for them.

The resident human has put sparkling, cool water into the bird bath which the Lorikeets take advantage of.

They drink, play and splash around, having a wonderful time.

The Lorikeets are spooked by a strange noise, they screech and fly into the trees.

Below in the garden they see, a very large unusual looking creature, chocolate brown in colour, with four legs, lots of curly fluff, long droopy ears, a brown nose and a long tail, but no eyes.

Another creature appears and starts chasing the brown one.

This one is different, it has four black legs with grey socks, is a lot smaller and has black straight fur with a grey collar.

There's a blaze of grey from the top of the head running in between the brown eyes to the black nose and around the jowls.

It has ears that stand straight up and a very short black tail.

The Lorikeets stay in the safety of the trees and observe these strange creatures invading their garden making a lot of noise, running around, growling, barking, rolling about in the grass and chewing on one another.

When the chocolate coloured creature is rolling over on its back they see it has eyes under the long fur on its' head.

The noisy creatures don't seem interested in the Lorikeets at all, so the Lorikeets quietly fly down to the trays and bird bath and again begin to eat and play in the water keeping an eye on the unusual invaders.

Again they are disturbed by another creature moving toward them.

The Lorikeets fly into the safety of the trees screeching their disapproval of their meal being disrupted once again.

They see this creature moves a lot slower than the other two. It doesn't make any sound and is a golden colour, has four legs, lots of fur but not curly and a long furry tail with a twist at the end.

It has a pink nose with some brown patches and two very long velvety ears that hang down either side of its' face. It looks around with soft, friendly brown eyes.

The other beasts run to the slow creature almost knocking it over and lick and kiss it gently on the face then continue to run around the garden playing with not a care in the world.

The Lorikeets return to the trays of seeds to continue their afternoon meal.

The chicks ask their mothers what the creatures are, Loretta and Rosanna explain they are domestic animals called dogs.

The resident human calls out "Jina, Johnson, Karmilla" and the brown fluffy one and the small black and grey dog race to the human.

The golden coloured dog is very slow and takes its' time, struggling to return.

The Lorikeets fly in and out of the garden at their leisure on a regular basis, no longer concerned about the resident dogs.

One day they notice the golden dog, Karmilla, isn't in the garden.

There is an extra tray with seeds placed high on a log in another part of the garden that has been freshly dug with new plants on display.

The invaders, Jina the Labradoodle and Johnson the Stumpy Tail Cattle Dog, are still in the garden running around, playing and rolling in the grass.

The Lorikeets fly onto the new tray to enjoy the seeds and continue to visit every day.

Lorikeet's Invaded by Furry Beasts

ISBN

978-1-7642196-1-7 (Paperback)

978-1-7642196-2-4 (eBook)

www.ingramcontent.com/pod-product-compliance
Lightning Source LLC
Chambersburg PA
CBHW060842270326
41933CB00002B/168

9 781764 219617